WOLFGANG AMADE

T0087081

SYMPHONY No. 40

G minor/g-Moll/sol mineur
K550

Edited by/Herausgegeben von
Richard Clarke

Ernst Eulenburg Ltd

London · Mainz · Madrid · New York · Paris · Prague · Tokyo · Toronto · Zürich

CONTENTS

The present edition of Mozart's Symphony No.40, K550, is based on
readings of the relevant texts published in *Wolfgang Amadeus Mozart:
Neue Ausgabe sämtlicher Werke*, IV/11.9

Ernst Eulenburg Ltd
48 Great Marlborough Street
London W1F 7BB

PREFACE

The Symphony in G minor, K550, was completed on 25 July 1788. The entry of this work in the chronological list *Verzeichnüß aller meiner Werke* that Mozart kept from February 1784 until November 1791 is immediately followed by another entry for 10 August recording the completion of the Symphony in C, K551, later known as the 'Jupiter' Symphony; only a few weeks earlier on 26 June the E flat Symphony, K543, had been listed. In a little over six weeks Mozart had written what were destined to be his last three symphonies, works which together with the 'Prague' Symphony represent his outstanding contributions to the form.

It is not known for what occasions these three masterpieces were composed: it is almost inconceivable that they would have been written without any prospect of their being performed. In the case of the G minor Symphony such a possibility is made all the more unlikely by reason of Mozart's later rescoring of the work. He would hardly have gone to the trouble of introducing clarinets and rewriting the oboe parts unless this revised version was due for performance. It may be that the three symphonies were to have been played at the series of concerts which Mozart was planning to hold in the new casino in Vienna in June 1788, but in the event the series did not take place. The Symphony in G minor could have been one of the two symphonies played at Mozart's Leipzig concert on 12 May 1789: or perhaps it may have been the 'Grand Symphony composed by Herr Mozart' included in the 'Grand Musical Concert' given on 16 April 1791 and repeated on the 17th by the Society of Musicians in aid of its widows and orphans. If this were the case – as Anton Stadler, Mozart's clarinettist friend, and his brother Johann took part in the concert – it is likely that the second version with clarinets would have been played. It is, of course, just possible that the prospects and hopes for the performance in Mozart's lifetime for one reason or another remained unrealised and he may never have heard his last three symphonies.

Mozart wrote over 50 symphonies, possibly as many as 60, if the works he put together from movements from his divertimentos and dramatic overtures are included. Most of the symphonies were composed before 1781 when he left the service of the Archbishop in Salzburg. The symphony at this time tended to be regarded less as a work of intrinsic importance than as the prelude to music of greater significance, whether opera or oratorio, or indeed the principal items in a concert programme. It is perhaps not surprising that in his early Vienna years Mozart was more interested in producing piano concertos, of which he wrote no fewer than 15 between 1782 and the end of 1786, for public performance by himself or his pupil, Babette Ployer. During the same period he wrote only three symphonies; of these the last, K504 in D, was composed in December 1786 for a performance in Prague on 19 January of the following year.

Of all the symphonies there are only two in minor keys, K550 and K183 also in G minor written in 1773. It is easy to exaggerate the significance for Mozart of the key of G minor, yet it does seem to have had a special meaning for him. Hermann Abert in his discussion of the opening scene of *Don Giovanni*[1] refers to G minor as 'die Tonart [...] des leidenschaftlichen Schmerzes' (the key of passionate grief) and certainly in the operas Mozart turns to G minor for those heart-rending outpourings of sorrow and despair that we find in Constanze's aria 'Traurigkeit' in *Die Entführung* or Pamina's 'Ach ich fühl's' in *Die Zauberflöte*. In the instrumental music, apart from the two symphonies, the Piano Quartet K478 of 1785 and the String Quintet K516 of 1787 are the only works written in this key but they too, especially the

---

[1] Hermann Abert, *W.A.Mozart* (Leipzig, ⁷1956), Vol.II, 396

Quintet, reflect some of this same emotional character.

It is not difficult to find an affinity of mood and character between the two G minor symphonies and certainly the excited syncopated quavers at the beginning of the earlier work in a way foreshadow the urgency of the opening of K550. There is moreover the same marked contrast between minuet and trio in both works: the strong unison opening of the earlier minuet standing out against the charm and grace of the trio for wind alone, while in the later work the strenuous contrapuntal clashes of the minuet are relieved by the gentle simplicity of the trio. Such parallels as these and the intensity of expression common to both works are clearly of interest, but it is the differences rather than the similarities that are more significant: above all it is Mozart's development as a composer and his new approach to the symphony that a comparison of the two works reveals. The 15 years which lay between their composition had seen an enormous enrichment of the emotional range and depth of the dramatic vocabulary which Mozart could draw upon to communicate his thoughts and feelings. There had been the production of the operas *Idomeneo* (1781), *Die Entführung aus dem Serail* (1782), *Le Nozze de Figaro* (1786) and *Don Giovanni* (1787) with their innumerable opportunities for the directly expressive use of harmonic and instrumental colour in the service of character drawing and stage action and atmosphere; there had been the transformation of the piano concerto from what had been primarily entertainment music into a work of high seriousness and dramatic potential; and in the chamber music, which included the six string quartets dedicated to Haydn and the string quintets in D, C and G minor, there had been the development of Mozart's ability to deploy his contrapuntal skill effectively within the framework of contemporary instrumental forms. The present work splendidly illustrates the harmonic boldness, contrapuntal mastery, adventurous exploration of tonality, as well as the telling use of instrumental colour of Mozart's mature style.

Ronald Woodham

VORWORT

Am 25. Juli 1788 war die g-Moll-Sinfonie, KV 550, fertiggestellt. Auf ihr Incipit im chronologischen *Verzeichnüß aller meiner Werke*, das Mozart von Februar 1784 bis November 1791 führte, folgt unmittelbar ein weiteres Incipit, das für den 10. August die Vollendung der später unter dem Namen „Jupiter-Sinfonie" bekannt gewordenen Sinfonie C-Dur, KV 551, anzeigt. Nur wenige Wochen zuvor ist unter dem 26. Juni die Es-Dur-Sinfonie, KV 543, angeführt. In etwas über sechs Wochen hat Mozart jene drei Sinfonien geschrieben, die seine letzten sein sollten – Werke, die mit der „Prager" für seinen herausragenden Beitrag zur Gattung Sinfonie stehen.

Zu welchen bestimmten Anlässen diese drei Meisterwerke komponiert wurden, weiß man nicht, doch geschah dies wohl kaum ohne irgendwelche Aussichten auf eine Aufführung, was im Falle der g-Moll-Sinfonie um so wahrscheinlicher ist, als Mozart die Partitur später umgearbeitet hat. Er hätte sich wohl kaum der Mühe unterzogen, Klarinettenstimmen hinzuzufügen und den Part der Oboen umzuschreiben, wenn es nicht für eine Aufführung beabsichtigt gewesen wäre. Vermutlich sollten die drei Sinfonien in einer Reihe von Konzerten vorgestellt werden, die Mozart für den Juni 1788 im Wiener neuen Casino geplant hatte. Doch diese Konzertreihe fand nie statt. Die g-Moll-Sinfonie könnte eine der beiden Sinfonien gewesen sein, die in Mozarts Leipziger Konzert am 12. Mai 1789 vorgetragen wurden. Vielleicht war die g-Moll-Sinfonie als „eine große Sinfonie von der Erfindung des Herrn Mozart" ein Programmpunkt der „großen musikalischen Akademie", die von der Wiener Tonkünstler-Sozietät am 16. April 1791 „zum Vortheile ihrer Wittwen und Waisen" gegeben und am 17. April wiederholt wurde. In diesem Falle dürfte die zweite Fassung mit Klarinetten gespielt worden sein, zumal Anton Stadler, Mozarts Freund, und dessen Bruder Johann als Klarinettisten an der Aufführung teilnahmen. Andererseits ist es durchaus möglich, dass Mozarts Erwartungen und Hoffnungen auf eine Aufführung aus unbekannten Gründen zu seinen Lebzeiten nicht in Erfüllung gingen und er somit seine letzten Sinfonien nie gehört hat.

Mozart schrieb mehr als fünfzig, vielleicht sogar sechzig Sinfonien, wenn man die Werke mitzählt, die er aus Einzelsätzen seiner Divertimenti und aus Ouvertüren zu Bühnenwerken zusammenfügte. Die Mehrzahl an Sinfonien komponierte er vor seinem Ausscheiden aus den Diensten des Salzburger Erzbischofs im Jahre 1781. Zu dieser Zeit wurde eine Sinfonie weniger als ein Werk von tieferer Bedeutung angesehen, als dass man sie als Vorspiel zur Musik von größerem Gewicht – etwa Oper, Oratorium oder eben als Hauptpunkt der Konzertprogramme – eingestuft hätte. So überrascht es nicht weiter, dass Mozart in seinen frühen Wiener Jahren mehr Interesse an der Komposition von Klavierkonzerten hatte. Zwischen 1782 und Ende 1786 schrieb er nicht weniger als fünfzehn Klavierkonzerte, die entweder von ihm oder seiner Schülerin Babette Ployer öffentlich aufgeführt wurden. Im gleichen Zeitraum schrieb er dagegen lediglich drei Sinfonien; die letzte von ihnen in D-Dur, KV 504, im Dezember 1786 komponiert, war für eine Aufführung in Prag am 19. Januar des folgenden Jahres bestimmt.

Von allen Sinfonien stehen überhaupt nur zwei in Moll, nämlich die Sinfonie KV 550 und die Sinfonie KV 183, ebenfalls in g-Moll, aus dem Jahre 1773. Die Gefahr, die Bedeutung der Tonart g-Moll bei Mozart zu überschätzen, ist groß; doch sieht es tatsächlich danach aus, als spiele sie eine besondere Rolle für ihn. Hermann Abert sieht in seiner Betrachtung der 1. Szene des *Don Giovanni*[1] g-Moll als „die Tonart [...] des leidenschaftlichen Schmerzes" an,

---

[1] Hermann Abert: *W. A. Mozart*, Leipzig ⁷1956, Band II, S. 396.

und gerade in seinen Opern überträgt Mozart der Tonart g-Moll jene ergreifenden Ausbrüche von Trauer und Verzweiflung wie Constanzes Arie „Traurigkeit" aus der *Entführung* oder Paminas „Ach ich fühl's" aus der *Zauberflöte*. Neben den genannten Sinfonien sind das Klavierquartett KV 478 von 1785 und das Streichquintett KV 516 von 1787 die einzigen Instrumentalwerke in dieser Tonart, und von ihnen spiegelt vor allem das Quintett die genannte Gefühlshaltung wider.

Die Gemeinsamkeiten zwischen den beiden g-Moll-Sinfonien in Stimmung und Charakter liegen auf der Hand und besonders die erregten synkopierten Viertelnoten zu Beginn des frühen Werkes lassen die eindringlichen Anfangstakte der Sinfonie KV 550 gewissermaßen vorausahnen. Darüber hinaus gibt es in beiden Werken den selben auffälligen Kontrast zwischen Menuett und Trio: Das herbe *unisono* zu Anfang des früheren Menuetts steht dem Charme und der Grazie des nur mit Bläsern besetzten Trios gegenüber, während im späteren Werk die unermüdliche kontrapunktische Verzahnung im Menuett zur Schlichtheit des Trios kontrastiert. Diese Parallelen und auch die beiden Sinfonien eigene Ausdrucksstärke sind zweifellos beachtenswert, doch springen die Unterschiede weit mehr ins Auge als die Gemeinsamkeiten: Es ist vor allem Mozarts Entwicklungsprozess als Komponist und seine neue Annäherung an die Gattung der Sinfonie, die im Vergleich der zwei genannten Werke zutage tritt. Während der fünfzehn Jahre zwischen der Entstehung der

beiden Sinfonien hatte die musikdramatische Sprache, derer sich Mozart bedienen konnte um seine Gedanken und Empfindungen mitzuteilen, eine erstaunliche Ausweitung an Ausdrucksnuancen und der emotionalen Intensität erfahren. Vorausgegangen waren die Opern *Idomeneo* (1781), *Die Entführung aus dem Serail* (1782), *Le Nozze di Figaro* (1786) und *Don Giovanni* (1787) mit zahllosen Gelegenheiten, unmittelbaren ausdrucksvollen Gebrauch von der harmonischen und instrumentalen Palette im Dienste der Charakterzeichnung, des Bühnengeschehens und der Atmosphäre zu machen; vorausgegangen war die Umformung des Klavierkonzertes aus dem ursprünglichen Bereich unterhaltender Musik in eine Komposition von großer Ernsthaftigkeit und dramatischem Potential; vorausgegangen war weiterhin in der Kammermusik mit den sechs Haydn gewidmeten Streichquartetten und den Streichquintetten in D-Dur, C-Dur und g-Moll die Weiterentwicklung von Mozarts Fähigkeit, seine kontrapunktischen Fertigkeiten im Rahmen der zeitgenössischen instrumentalen Formen wirksam einzusetzen. Das vorliegende Werk legt auf eindrucksvolle Weise von der harmonischen Kühnheit, kontrapunktischer Meisterschaft, dem die Grenzen der Tonalität streifenden Wagemut und auch dem wirkungsvollen Einsatz der Klangfarbe in Mozarts Spätstil Zeugnis ab.

Ronald Woodham
Übersetzung: Norbert Henning

PRÉFACE

La Symphonie en *sol* mineur, K.550, fut achevée le 25 juillet 1788. L'inscription de cette œuvre dans la liste chronologique *Verzeichnüß aller meiner Werke*, établie par Mozart de février 1784 à novembre 1791, fut suivie immédiatement par celle, le 10 août, de la Symphonie en *ut*, K.551, connue plus tard comme la Symphonie « Jupiter ». La Symphonie en *mi* bémol, K.543, y avait été cataloguée seulement quelques semaines auparavant. En un peu plus de six semaines, Mozart a donc écrit les œuvres qui seraient ses dernières symphonies et qui constituent, avec la Symphonie « Prague », ses contributions les plus saisissantes à cette forme.

On ignore à quelle occasion furent composés ces trois chefs-d'œuvre mais il est presque inconcevable qu'ils eussent été écrits sans projet d'exécution. Dans le cas de la Symphonie en *sol* mineur, cette possibilité paraît d'autant plus improbable du fait de la ré-instrumentation ultérieure à laquelle procéda Mozart. Il ne serait sûrement pas donné la peine d'introduire des clarinettes et de réécrire les parties de hautbois sans avoir en vue une exécution de cette version révisée. Il se peut que ces trois symphonies aient été destinées à la série de concerts, qui n'eut finalement pas lieu, prévue par Mozart en juin 1788 au nouveau casino de Vienne. La Symphonie en *sol* mineur fut peut-être l'une de celles jouées au concert donné par Mozart à Leipzig le 12 mai 1789 ou la « Grande symphonie composée par Herr Mozart » figurant au programme du « Grand Concert Musical » donné le 16 avril 1791 et repris le 17 par la Société des Musiciens au profit de ses veuves et orphelins. En ce cas, Anton Stadler, ami clarinettiste de Mozart, et son frère Johann ayant participé à ce concert, il est probable qu'y fut jouée la deuxième version avec clarinettes de la symphonie. Il se peut également toutefois que, pour diverses raisons, projets et espoirs d'exécution n'aient pu se réaliser du vivant de Mozart et qu'il n'ait donc jamais entendu ses trois dernières symphonies.

Mozart composa plus de cinquante symphonies, une soixantaine si l'on y inclut les œuvres qu'il assembla à partir de mouvements de ses *divertimenti* et de ses ouvertures dramatiques. Ses symphonies furent, pour la plupart, composées avant 1781, date à laquelle il quitta le service de l'archevêque de Salzbourg. La tendance de l'époque était moins de considérer la symphonie comme une œuvre d'importance intrinsèque ou comme la partie essentielle d'un programme de concert que comme le prélude à d'autres œuvres plus importantes, opéra ou oratorio. Il n'est donc pas étonnant qu'au cours de ses premières années à Vienne, Mozart se soit plutôt tourné vers le concerto pour piano – il n'en écrivit pas moins de quinze entre 1782 et la fin de 1786 en vue d'exécutions en public par lui-même ou par son élève Babette Ployer – alors que, pendant la même période, il ne composa que trois symphonies, dont la dernière, K.504 en *ré*, achevée en décembre 1786, fut donnée à Prague le 19 janvier de l'année suivante.

De toutes les symphonies de Mozart, deux seulement sont en mode mineur, la Symphonie K.550 et la Symphonie K.183 de 1773, également en *sol* mineur. Sans vouloir trop facilement exagérer la portée de la tonalité de *sol* mineur pour Mozart, il semble néanmoins qu'il y ait trouvé un certain sens. Hermann Abert, dans une analyse de la première scène de *Don Giovanni*, désigne *sol* mineur comme « *die Tonart* [...] *des leidenschaftlichen Schmerzes* » (La tonalité de la douleur passionnée). Il est certain que, dans ses opéras, Mozart recourt à *sol* mineur pour exprimer les chagrins déchirants, comme dans l'air de Constance « Traurigkeit » de *Die Entführung* ou dans celui de Pamina « Ach ich fühl's » de *Die Zauberflöte*. Dans sa musique

---

[1] Hermann Abert, *W.A.Mozart* (Leipzig, [7]1956), Vol. II, 396

instrumentale, à côté des deux symphonies, le Quatuor avec piano K.478 de 1785 et le Quintette à cordes K.516 de 1787, seules œuvres empruntant cette tonalité, dégagent en partie, surtout le Quintette, le même caractère émotionnel.

On perçoit une affinité de climat et de manière entre les deux symphonies en *sol* mineur, les croches syncopées frénétiques du début de la plus ancienne annonçant l'urgence du début du K.550. Il existe, de plus, le même contraste marqué entre le menuet et le *trio* dans les deux œuvres : le vigoureux unisson ouvrant le premier menuet s'opposant au charme et à la grâce du *trio* instrumenté pour les seuls instruments à vent, tandis que, dans la deuxième symphonie, les frottements contrapuntiques et opiniâtres du menuet sont allégés par la douce simplicité du *trio*. L'intérêt présenté par ces parallèles et par l'intensité similaire habitant les deux œuvres est indéniable mais les différences qui les distinguent s'avèrent encore plus révélatrices que leurs ressemblances. En effet, leur comparaison dévoile avant tout l'évolution de Mozart compositeur et sa nouvelle approche de la forme symphonique. Les quinze années séparant leurs deux compositions virent un immense enrichissement de la palette émotionnelle et de la profondeur du vocabulaire dramatique sur lesquelles Mozart pouvait s'appuyer pour donner forme à ses pensées et sentiments. Il y eut la production des opéras *Idomeneo* (1781), *Die Entführung aus dem Serail* (1782), *Le Nozze di Figaro* (1786) et *Don Giovanni* (1787) qui fournirent à Mozart d'innombrables occasions de se servir de façon immédiatement expressive du coloris harmonique et instrumental pour caractériser personnages, intrigue et atmosphère. Il y eut la transformation du concerto pour piano de musique de divertissement en œuvre chargée de gravité et de potentiel dramatique. Il y eut, enfin, dans sa musique de chambre, comprenant les six quatuors à cordes dédiés à Haydn et les quintettes en *ré*, en *ut* et en *sol* mineur, l'essor de l'aptitude de Mozart à déployer son talent contrapuntique dans le cadre de formes instrumentales contemporaines. Cette symphonie illustre superbement la hardiesse harmonique, la maîtrise contrapuntique, l'exploration intrépide de la tonalité ainsi que l'utilisation audacieuse de la couleur instrumentale du style de la maturité de Mozart.

Ronald Woodham
Traduction : Agnès Ausseur

SYMPHONY No. 40

Wolfgang Amadeus Mozart
(1756–1791)
K550

I. Molto Allegro

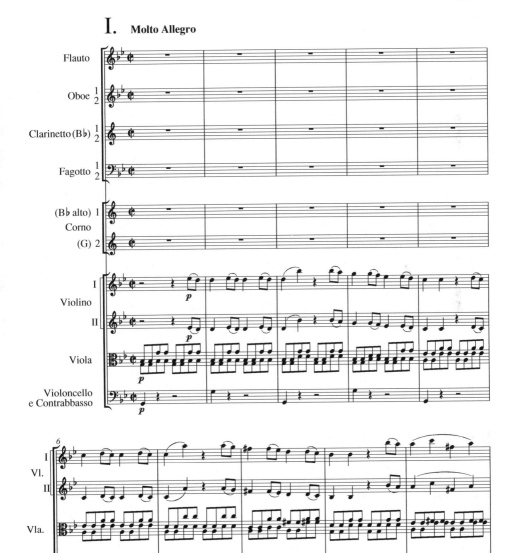

Edited by Richard Clarke
© 2012 Ernst Eulenburg Ltd, London
and Ernst Eulenburg & Co GmbH, Mainz

4

6

10

12

14

21

24

26

II. Andante

28

34

III. Menuetto

Allegretto

42

44

D.C. Menuetto

46

IV. **Allegro assai**

55

56

58

64